Animals All Around

Do Bees Make Butter?

A Book About Things Animals Make

by Michael Dahl

Illustrated by Todd Ouren

Special thanks to our advisers for their expertise:

Kathleen E. Hunt, Ph.D.
Research Scientist & Lecturer, Zoology Department
University of Washington, Seattle, Washington

Susan Kesselring, M.A., Literacy Educator
Rosemount-Apple Valley-Eagan (Minnesota) School District

PICTURE WINDOW BOOKS
MINNEAPOLIS, MINNESOTA

Managing Editor: Bob Temple
Creative Director: Terri Foley
Editor: Peggy Henrikson
Editorial Adviser: Andrea Cascardi
Copy Editor: Laurie Kahn
Designer: Todd Ouren
Page production: BANTA Digital Group
The illustrations in this book were rendered digitally.

Picture Window Books
5115 Excelsior Boulevard
Suite 232
Minneapolis, MN 55416
1-877-845-8392
www.picturewindowbooks.com

Printed in the United States of America.

Library of Congress Cataloging-in-Publication Data
Dahl, Michael.
Do bees make butter? : a book about things animals make / by Michael Dahl ;
illustrated by Todd Ouren.
p. cm. — (Animals all around)
Summary: Introduces a number of different animals and what they produce.
Includes bibliographical references and index.
ISBN 1-4048-0288-6 (Reinforced Library Binding)
1. Animal behavior—Juvenile literature. [1. Animal behavior.]
I. Ouren, Todd, ill. II. Title.
QL751.5 .D328 2004
591.5—dc22
2003016525

Do bees make butter?

No! Bees make honey.

Honeybees make honey from sweet liquid called nectar that they drink from flowers. The nectar mixes with special juices from the bees' bodies. Back at their hives, the bees store the sweet liquid in honeycombs. The liquid dries as thick, golden honey.

4

Do caterpillars make butter?

No! Caterpillars make cocoons.

Squirmy caterpillars spin cocoons around their bodies. They spin with silky threads that come from their mouths. Hidden within their cocoons, the caterpillars slowly change shape. One day, out flutter soft moths or bright butterflies!

Do oysters make butter?

No! Oysters make pearls.

Sometimes a grain of sand slips inside an oyster's shell. Ouch! The oyster quickly covers the sand with a liquid. The shiny liquid thickens and hardens. Soon a gleaming pearl is formed around the grain of sand.

8

Do wasps make butter?

No! Wasps make paper.

A wasp's sharp jaws scrape bits of wood from trees, poles, or fences. The wood mixes with saliva in the insect's mouth and becomes soft. The wasp spits and spreads this mixture in thin layers to form a nest. The layers dry into soft but tough paper.

10

Do beavers make butter?

No! Beavers make dams.

Beavers cut down small trees with their sharp front teeth. They build a wall of trees, twigs, and mud in a flowing stream. The wall becomes a dam that slows down the stream and makes a pool. Beavers swim and build their homes in the new pool.

Do weaverbirds make butter?

No! Weaverbirds make giant nests.

Weaverbirds gather strands of grass and straw. They fly to a tall, sturdy tree. Carefully, their busy beaks weave and knot the strands together. Hundreds of weavers weave a single giant nest. One nest can hold 300 pairs of birds, and each pair has its own entrance.

Do termites make butter?

No! Termites make mounds.

African termites build huge mounds from soil and saliva.
They dig tunnels and chimneys in the mounds to let hot air escape.
Deep inside the mound, termites keep cool and comfortable.

Do spiders make butter?

No! Spiders make webs.

A spider's body makes silky threads that the spider weaves into a web. Strong, sticky webs catch unlucky bugs that become the spider's feast. Webs also catch the morning dew and sparkle in the sun.

Do bowerbirds make butter?

No! Bowerbirds make decorations.

The male satin bowerbird collects blue and yellow objects. He looks for things such as feathers, flowers, and blue beetle shells. The bird carefully decorates the ground near his nest, or bower. He uses his treasures to attract curious female bowerbirds flying overhead.

Do people make butter?

Yes! People make butter.

People make butter by whipping up, or churning, rich milk. They get the milk from cows, goats, sheep, or yaks. People spread butter on bread or on pancakes. They drizzle it on popcorn and add it when they bake. All around the world, people make and eat butter.

What Animals Make

Some animals make soft things.

caterpillars	cocoons
wasps	paper

Some animals make shiny things.

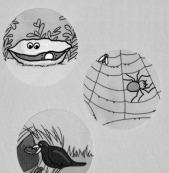

oysters	pearls
spiders	webs
bowerbirds	decorations

Some animals make big things.

beavers	dams
weaverbirds	nests
termites	mounds

Some animals make tasty things.

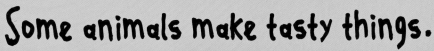

bees	honey

Glossary

caterpillar—a young butterfly or moth that is in the stage of growth when it looks like a worm with legs. Some caterpillars are fuzzy or colorful.

churn—to stir up something quickly and roughly. People churn rich milk or cream to make it thick and turn it into butter.

cocoon—a covering made by a caterpillar to protect itself as it changes into a butterfly or moth

decorations—pretty, shiny, or colorful things that are used to make some thing or place look nice

maze—a network of tunnels or paths that connect with one another

nectar—a sweet liquid found inside flowers. Bees use nectar to make honey.

pearl—a hard, round, shiny object made inside an oyster. Pearls are used in valuable jewelry.

saliva—spit, or juices in an animal's mouth

Index

To Learn More

At the Library

Christian, Eleanor, and Lyzz Roth-Singer. *Let's Make Butter.* Mankato, Minn.: Yellow Umbrella Books, 2001.

Hartley, Karen, Chris Macro, and Philip Taylor. *Caterpillar.* Des Plaines, Ill.: Heinemann Library, 1999.

Milton, Joyce. *Honeybees.* New York: Grosset & Dunlap, 2003.

Schaefer, Lola M. *Spiders: Spinners and Trappers.* Mankato, Minn.: Bridgestone Books, 2001.

Sullivan, Jody. *Beavers: Big-Toothed Builders.* Mankato, Minn.: Bridgestone Books, 2003.

On the Web

Fact Hound offers a safe, fun way to find Web sites related to this book. All of the sites on Fact Hound have been researched by our staff.
http://www.facthound.com

1. Visit the Fact Hound home page.
2. Enter a search word related to this book, or type in this special code: 1404802886.
3. Click on the FETCH IT button.

Your trusty Fact Hound will fetch the best sites for you!